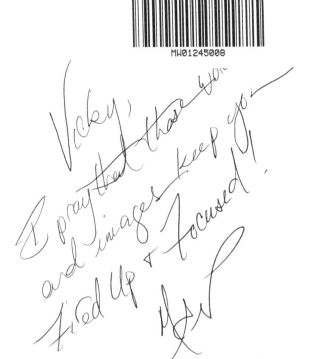

Vicky,
I pray that these words
and images keep you
fired up & focused!

Fired Up

&

Focused!

Lessons on life,
faith and business
from Philip Simmons

The Village Blacksmith

Fired Up

& Focused!

*Lessons on life,
faith and business
from Philip Simmons*

The Village Blacksmith

ARMOUR OF LIGHT
PUBLISHING
Chapel Hill, North Carolina · Charleston, South Carolina

Published in the United States of America by
Armour of Light Publishing
P.O. Box 778
Chapel Hill, North Carolina 27514
(919) 536 - 9375
Visit us at: www.armouroflight.org

Design by Michael E. Evans

ISBN 978-0-9817120-9-3

LCCN 2009905557

First Edition

All scriptures quoted from the Authorized King James Version unless otherwise noted.

10 9 8 7 6 5 4 3 2 *1*

PHILIP SIMMONS
Master Blacksmith
June 9, 1912 - June 22, 2009

*"If you want your prayers answered,
get up off your knees and hustle."*

Philip Simmons

Photo by Claire Y. Greene

Philip Simmons is, without question, the most celebrated of all Charleston iron-workers. Born June 9, 1912 on Daniel Island, Mr. Simmons moved to Charleston in 1919. He attended Buist Elementary School (now Buist Academy) but received his most important education from local blacksmith, Peter Simmons.

It was in Peter Simmons' shop on Calhoun Street that Philip Simmons acquired the values and refined the talents that would distinguish him from others who labored in the blacksmith trade. I hope you will glean insights of value from this small glimpse of my short time with this great servant.

I've never met anyone quite like Philip Simmons, but I have been drawn to the character traits that make him special most of my life. I love his sense of humor and the self-deprecating manner that causes him not to take himself too seriously. I envy his great appreciation for what many would consider an unimportant or even undesirable talent. Philip Simmons has truly made the most of what God gave him.

He is enterprising. He finds a way to apply his gift to almost everything around him and he makes things happen. He walks by faith with a heavy emphasis on the walk. And Mr. Simmons cares. Caring is such a rare and often ridiculed quality in today's self-absorbed world. Caring is costly. Caring induces pain that could be easily avoided. Caring involves those who dare to do it in difficulties that others easily pass by.

But Philip Simmons has not just passed by. His mark is made all over Charleston and in other parts of the world. Not just the mark of his re-markable ironwork. I'm talking about the mark of his heart. Kind words. Faith filled prayers. Infectious smiles. Uncelebrated gifts. All these and more have earned Mr. Simmons a perma-nent place in my heart. I hope this little book will earn him a similar place in yours.

Table Of Contents

How This Book Works

How This Book Works

- Information
- Art
- Practical Principles

Mr. Simmons at work in the shop.

This book was written with three fundamental purposes in mind. First of all I want you to know about Philip Simmons. Not Just his work, but the man himself. It has been said that Alexander the Great's primary motivation for conquering the world was to make everyone aware of the teachings of Aristotle and Plato. Well, we are not looking to conquer the world. But I do believe that Mr. Simmons has made the world a better place and I want you to know about his contribution.

Alexis De Tocqueville, in his *Democracy In America,* said of Americans: *"They will habitually prefer the useful to the beautiful and they will require that the beautiful be useful."* Mr. Simmons has transformed the craft of blacksmithing into an art form. He makes things of beauty that are practical as well.

Mr. Simmons has indeed made the useful beautiful. I hope you find this book beautiful and useful as well: easy to read, pleasant to look at and handle. And most important of all, I hope that the practical principles found inside will help you with your life and business.

The cover page to each chapter will contain bullet points. Use them as motivators for yourself, your family, your church, or your team.

The Work
Will Speak
For Itself

Q&A

- What are you working on?
- What is your work saying?
- What have you created that would raise you from the dead?

I had heard of Philip Simmons. But to be perfectly honest, I can't tell you where or from whom. All the locals know him. It's newcomers (comeyahs) like me who are ignorant of this national treasure. I'm certain someone told me about him, but it feels more like the information was just in the air. It's as though his name was part of the landscape or the infrastructure. And that makes perfect sense to me now.

Mr. Simmons has over seven hundred works of art (gates, grates, grills, etc.) around the city of Charleston. It makes even more sense, now that I've finally gotten to know him a little better. Especially since I heard him say,

"I love to hear the iron sing."

And sing it does. Not just the ringing of that curiously small hammer on the well worn anvil he bought over fifty years ago when he works. The work takes on a life of its own and continues to sing to all who pass by.

Surely, the work is speaking--*singing*--for itself.

There is a woman in the Bible by the name of Tabitha or Dorcas. She was a seamstress and she was well known for her craftsmanship and her generosity. There came a time when she got sick and died. Upon notice of her death, those who had benefited from her labor of love cried out to God and sent for Peter, the apostle. He responded to the call and was met with a great display of the work that this great woman had produced. He proceeded to pray and God raised the woman from the dead.

Whenever I read this account, I think of people like Mr. Simmons who have poured so much of themselves into their work and, through it, the lives of others. It inspires me to strive for, excellence and to increase my liberality. These two very natural acts often produce supernatural results.

Begin With His Grandmother

*"To reform a man,
you must begin with his grandmother."*

Victor Hugo

Q&A

- Who are your greatest influences?
- You are the company.
- What fundamentals drive your business?

When I finally got to meet Mr. Simmons, I was surprised at how small he was. I was surprised at how simple and small his house and shop were too. That notwithstanding, I was pleasantly surprised at how inviting and engaging he had managed to remain.

He took us into his makeshift office, crammed with memorabilia from years of work and service. There were pictures of the mayor, a governor, a senator, and one with President Reagan alongside accolades and honors of every order. But he passed over all of them and directed our attention to something far more important.

"You see that picture right there?" he said, pointing with a stick. *"I bet you don't know who that is? "* I took the telling lines of my opening monologue in the play *Sermon of Fire* directly from that first meeting with Mr. Simmons.

"Why that been my grandmother." He continued with nary a pause. *"I was born in her house on Daniel Island, 88 year ago. "*

He said it with such affection, pride and authority. He said it with emphasis, as something that should never be overlooked or forgotten. He made it clear that his work ethic, his values and his love for people and learning began there - with his grandmother.

It brought back memories of my own paternal grandma Bea, who taught me that life is without boundaries for me. She showed me that practical faith, good manners, articulate speech and productive enterprise would open any door. I witnessed all of the above in action as we traveled from state to state on Greyhound buses and she shopped along side wealthy white women at The Proctor Shoppe and other "exclusive" venues, long before the Civil Rights Bill was signed into law.

What's In A Name?

*"A good name is better than
precious ointment ... "*

Ecclesiastes 7:1a

Q&A

- Where did your name come from?
- What does your name mean?
- What gives value to your name?

Mr. Simmons' Aunt Estelle

Right beside the picture of his grandmother was another photo from the same era; He continued this most intimate of tours with the commentary, *"You see that one behind her? That's her sister, my Aunt Estelle."* Then he made a critical distinction.

> *"Most people think it was my grandmother that gave me this name I got--Philip but she don't.*
>
> *No. That been my Aunt Estelle. And you know where she got it? She got it right out the Bible. "*

Now, Mr. Simmons is a man of great practical faith. He has been an active member of St. John's Reformed Episcopal Church for over eighty years. He believes in prayer, but he is also firmly committed to self-reliance. His "favorite" motto is:

> *"If you want your prayers answered, get off your knees and hustle."*

The name Philip *"from the Bible"* fits him perfectly. It is Greek in origin and means Lover or Lover of horses. Mr. Simmons spent much of his youth shoeing horses. The biblical Philip was an early disciple of Jesus and went and got his brother Nathaniel and brought him to Jesus as well. Time will only tell how many people have been brought to faith and faithfulness by Mr. Simmons' practical faith. He finished his commentary with one lasting remark.

"That name don 't mean nothing
if you ain't got a dollar in your pocket. "

The chuckle at the end of that comment let me know that Philip Simmons is not one to rest on his laurels. He is a business man. And all businessmen know that business is about what you're doing, not what you've done. Before we left, he had sold me an autographed copy of John Michael Vlach's book, *Charleston Blacksmith*. I had a copy of Philip Simmons' name. Mr. Simmons had some of my dollars in his pocket.

Note: I actually thought that Mr. Simmons may have adopted his surname from Peter Simmons, but those close to him assure me that this was not the case.

Starting A Fire

Starting A Fire

- Start Small
- Use what's available
- Make sure things are in place
- Timing is critical
- Be patient
- Leave it alone

Mr. Simmons at work near his home made forge.

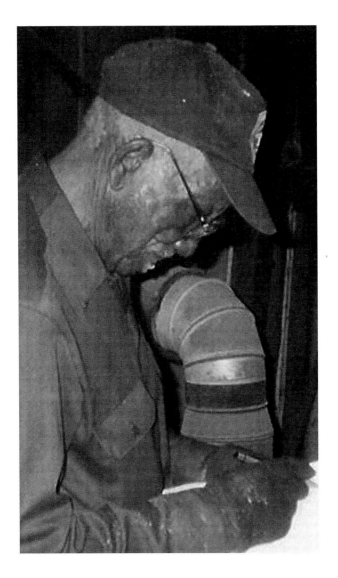

After showing us much of his memorabilia (the makeshift desk that had been his wife Ertha's dresser, drawings from gates that now grace grand buildings, pictures of priests and presidents, awards and accolades too numerous to mention), he took us around the back of the house to the shop.

On the way, I noticed him picking up debris. At first, I thought he was just tidying up, which seemed somewhat hopeless. I mean, it's a true craftsman's yard. There is what we would consider junk everywhere: Scraps of metal and unfinished projects. Mistakes and rejects. Found objects and so much bric a brac.

He picked up a stick here and a scrap of paper there all the way to the shop. And when we got in the shop, he began to build a fire. It was not something he stopped to do, however. It was more like second nature, he kept talking to us. His eyes remained firmly focused.

He never drew attention to the fact that he was building a fire. He just did it. And it wasn't like any fire I had ever built.

First of all, the flame was small, just a hand full of twigs and paper. Secondly, there was a simple order to that fire accompanied by an experienced sense of timing. He knew what to put where and when. Thirdly and most importantly, he didn't meddle with it. He knew how to leave it alone and let it burn. Consequently, unlike me, he didn't have to do it again.

Philip Simmons knows how to build a fire. And not just in a forge. A forge and electric bellows, I might add, he was proud to note that he had built himself.

Bus Pass

Character of Iron

- Get up & Go
- Ask for help
- Don't be overly dependent

The old craftsman in the shop yard. Photo by Steve Lepre.

That first visit to Mr. Simmons' home ended much too soon. As we (the cast of *Sermon Of Fire*) made our way to our cars parked on Blake Street, I noticed that he was tagging along. I turned to say a final goodbye and he seemed to want something more. I inquired if I could take him somewhere and his eyes lit up. *"I want to go to Wendy's to get some vegetables,"* he said. I found out later that "vegetables" really meant French Fries. I was elated. I was going to get to share a meal with this living legend and hopefully get a further glimpse into Charleston's past.

He settled into my old convertible, casually commenting on a Chrysler he once owned, and off we went to Wendy's. He gave great directions, well aware of potential traffic delays. When we got to the restaurant, I parked the car and proceeded to get out. At which point he bid me a definitive farewell. I indicated that I was prepared to dine with him, and he politely but firmly declined my imposing invitation. I was confused as well as disappointed.

"How will you get home?" I inquired. It was then that I discovered what may be Philip Simmons' most powerful characteristic. He replied: *"I've got a Bus Pass. Hmmmph. You can get all over this town for a quarter."* And get all over this town (and this country) he does. Anyone who ever just dropped by $30^{1/2}$ Blake Street and tried to catch Philip Simmons at home knows what I mean.

Mr. Simmons doesn't live at $30^{1/2}$ Blake Street anymore. Both the house and the shop have been turned into museums. But the memory of a man who made an indelible mark on his neighborhood, his city, and his world, will live forever at those and other historic landmarks.

Write three things you could do, change or improve that would make your life better and/or get you closer to your goal(s).

1.

2.

3.

I got the opportunity to meet Mr. Simmons as a result of a play, *"Sermon of Fire"* (See page 87) that was written about him by a Charleston high school drama teacher and one of her students. On opening night, he was there with much of his family. Opening nights are always nerve wracking, but on this one, my primary concern was that Mr. Simmons would be pleased with my characterization of him. The cast got a standing ovation and then the real show began.

It was amazing to watch the crowd of people gather around him. It was even more amazing to see how he worked that crowd. Signing autographs, taking pictures, remembering names and inquiring about family members. When I finally got close enough to get his attention, I just had to know, *"How did I do?"* He thought and then replied with a mischievous smile; *"I'll give you 99% percent. That way you'll know there is always room for improvement."*

Never before have I so greatly appreciated or better understood a critical compliment.

Mr. Simmons is always improving. At 91 he was still looking for new ways to better his craft. He observes the work of others with keen interest, and he is not afraid to tackle the unknown.

My wife and I were driving through Charleston one Mother's Day after church and spotted Mr. Simmons meandering down King Street. We stopped and beckoned him and he was as glad as ever to see a familiar face. We asked what he was doing and he replied:

"Just checking out the city. They've added some new things and I have to keep up with what s going on."

He had actually been up to a rooftop cafe just to get a better look. He joined us for lunch and even tried to pay the bill. And when we started to take him home, he insisted on being dropped at a sick church member's home for a visit. Philip Simmons just keeps getting better day by day.

"I Wanted To Quit"

Don't Quit

- Conditions Change, Success Principles Do Not
- Don't Let Tradition Trump Opportunity

The Fan Gate • Photo by Claire Y. Greene

It is important to note that the work of Philip Simmons was not done in some artistic, vacuum. Born in 1912, Mr. Simmons has weathered economic downturns, personal debt, wars, and racism at its best/worst. The one thing that he has survived, that so many others do not, is change.

He told me about the time he thought of giving up the blacksmith trade. When the automobile showed up, the demand for horse shoes and most things equine all but dried up. But, ever creative, he began making minor repairs to existing ironwork around town and crafting hitches to attach vender wagons to the automobile. Then the large chains like Sears and Montgomery Ward started manufacturing those wagon hitches faster and cheaper. I doubt very seriously, however, that they could make them any better.

So, the man who has decorated Charleston decided to hang up his hammer and abandon his anvil. Then a curious thing happened. A local resident, Jack Krawcheck, asked if Mr. Simmons could build a decorative wrought iron gate from a crude sketch. Mr. Simmons still has that sketch. He had never done anything like it before. He told me, *"that man had more confidence in me than I had in myself."*

Mr. Simmons built two gates and a grill that are still at 311-313 King Street today. To say "the rest is history" would be one of the world's great understatements. That iron work will outlast us all.

It is hard to imagine now that quitting ever crossed Mr. Simmons' mind. But that's what makes him so special. We all think of quitting from time to time and many of us have done so. Not only have we quit doing, we have often quit dreaming. Dreaming is one thing, however, that one simply cannot help but do while in the presence of Philip Simmons. I'm glad he didn't quit. I'm just as glad to know that he remains transparent enough to let me know he thought about it.

Too Busy

Are You Too Busy

- Cherish your relationships
- Work on things you care about
- Take in a ball game or two

Enter In • Photo by Claire Y. Greene

Mr. Simmons' wife, Ertha, died after a six week illness when her third child, Lillian, was just a toddler. Philip & Ertha Simmons were married for four short years. Mr. Simmons never remarried. I have often imagined how he must have loved her and marveled at his resolve to remain single for over sixty-five years. One day, having no such resolve of my own, I had to ask why.

He laughed and assured me that there had been a few *"girlfriends"* since Ertha passed but none of them lasted long. One girlfriend actually told him, *"Philip, you're too busy to be my boyfriend. I need a beau that can take me to the dance and to the show."* So, the ever resourceful Philip Simmons responded by finding her a boyfriend. *"And I found her a good one too,"* he will tell you with pride. Nothing but the best for Philip Simmons *(The Village Matchmaker?)*

He admits he was too busy. What with demand growing for his iron work, his church life, his volunteer work with the Boy Scouts (he was a troup leader for years), the YMCA and the YWCA *(of which he is still a member)* and various other community and personal involvements, there was just no time to replace Ertha. And I wonder if she *could* be replaced.

Few people can keep up with Philip Simmons. He is a force of nature that is rare among men, to say the least.

Philip Simmons is a dynamic community treasure who prefers to spend his time dreaming and drawing, meeting and making new friends, enlightening and entertaining neighborhood kids. If you can catch him, he still enjoys a good baseball game. But ladies, don't expect any extra innings.

First & Last

Have you got the Spark?

- What interests you?
- Who inspires you?
- Whom do you inspire?

On more than one occasion, I've noticed that when Mr. Simmons attends a performance of *Sermon Of Fire*, he is, without fail, the first to arrive and the last to leave. His appearances seem driven by something far more powerful than mere social obligation however. He remains youthful, even childlike in his eagerness. *(A characterization I use with the utmost respect, aspiring to win back the jaded areas of my own heart that I glibly euphemize with misnomers like experience, wisdom and age.)* Mr. Simmons has maintained that most curious and coveted quality of remaining genuinely interested.

He greeted me after a performance at his church once and encouraged me with a smile. *"You've still got the spark,"* he said. I really hope I do. In this age of mass produced, cookie cutter, what's new, melodrama, I would be satisfied with a glowing ember that someone might stir up or blow on.

When I was a kid, my maternal grandma, Jessie, had a pot bellied stove in her kitchen. She would leave it burning with a tea kettle on top to regulate the humidity while we went out on brisk Virginia mornings. Ever fascinated by fire, I would run to the stove when we returned and report to grandma that the fire had *"gone out."*

She would smile as she reached for the poker and assured me that it had not. Then she would stir up those embers as she discarded any debris from our adventures into the old stove. And with a gentle breath of life, she could always turn what seemed dead into a raging blaze again.

That's what Philip Simmons has done for me. He has stirred me up. He has blown a breath of fresh air into what could have easily become a cool existence. He has taken what I may have often mistaken for useless debris and used it as fuel for a useful fire. I call it a useful fire, because for him, like my grandma, the fire remains merely a tool. It is not the objective.

The zest and zeal that Mr. Simmons maintains is there to heat up and soften an increasingly cold, hard world. Once heated up, he can bend it and shape it into a thing of resilient beauty. I for one

Michael E. Evans

am glad to have been the subject of his interest for a season, because he does indeed, *still have the spark.*"

Michael E. Evans

2001
A Space Odyssey

A Room With A View

- What is your gift?
- Who, can use your gift?
- Are you making room for your gift?

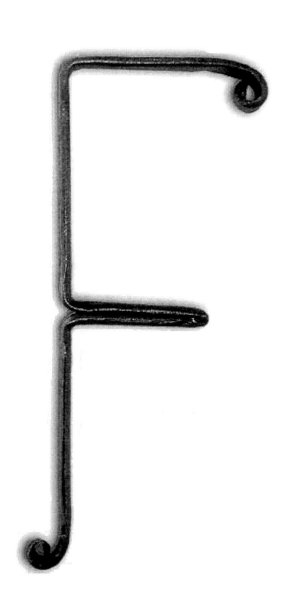

Michael E. Evans

Proverbs 18:16 says; *"A man's gift makes room for him and brings him before great men."* Philip Simmons is living proof of this great truth. But to know him is to know that he too has made room for his gift.

Mr. Simmons used to tell me that he was retired and didn't work in the shop anymore, but that was not altogether true. On a lonely back wall in his cluttered shop hung some iron letters. Prior to the turn of the century, Philip Simmons wanted to commemorate the *"special day."* So he went in his shop and began to fashion iron letters *(actually initials of clients, family members, and friends)* imprinted with the date 1/1/2000 and his signature -- **PS**.

Unfortunately, Mr. Simmons became ill in the process and could not finish on time. But his customers, realizing the value of the work and the heart behind the effort, assured him that they wanted those letters whenever he could get them done, as long as they were signed and dated. The last time I saw him, Philip Simmons was still working on those letters. He made a few full sets and gave them away to people he had promised to make something for through the years.

Perhaps the most critical piece of information here is that Mr. Simmons was still working. Whether it be the manual labor of bending iron or the great work of shaping hearts, he never just took up space.

South Carolina's senior senator, Strom Thurmond worked until he was 99 years old. He died six months after he retired. For over fifty years, legendary comedian, George Burns, invited people to his 100th birthday celebration at the London Palladium. Burns actually had the Palladium booked for that day but was too ill to perform when the date arrived. He died less than six months later.

These men and more like them, stood before multitudes, great and small, because they had peculiar gifts. Their gifts made room for them and they found space for their gifts.

Sermon Of Fire

Sermon Of Fire

- What pressures do you face?
- What connection do you have with the next generation?
- How have you positioned your enterprise to inspire?

Michael E. Evans

As I mentioned earlier, I got the opportunity to meet Mr. Simmons as a result of a play that was written about his life. A modern day parable, *Sermon of Fire* tells the story of the relationship between Breezy, a young girl, and her grandfather, Philip Simmons.

Breezy struggles with the pressures of being a teenager while Philip, amid growing personal debts, searches for a new and meaningful way to communicate with, his granddaughter and do business in a changing world. This play examines the special bond between youth and old age and the power of enterprise to inspire.

Mr. Simmons has been such a great inspiration to me that I have taken many of the principles I gleaned from our encounters and applied them to my various training seminars and motivational speeches. After noticing so many of them pop up unrehearsed, I decided to gather them all together for something new. I call this collection of principles *Fired Up & Focused!*

Fired Up & Focused! is a modular *(to accommodate time and budget constraints)* business training seminar designed to help you and your team zero in on what is really important and maintain the zest and enthusiasm to get from idea to prototype to product to profitability as quickly as possible.

I hope this little book has been an inspiration to you. My goal is simple: We at 2nd Ending Communications are here to help you achieve your goals. With this powerful mixture of motivation, information, and the inspiration of a living master craftsman, you can't help but leave *Fired Up & Focused!*

If you want more information about how to get your team *Fired Up & Focused!*, call, write, or e-mail:

Michael E. Evans
Second Ending Communications
P.O. Box 778
Chapel Hill, NC 27514
(919) 572-2808 / (919) 536-9375
michael@focusedfire.com

Acknowledgments

There are a few key people that made Mr. Simmons' great impact on my life and this little book possible. I would like to take a moment to thank each of them for their part in helping me to get to know The Village Blacksmith.

Lesly Jacobs Lamb, author of *Sermon Of Fire*, director, friend and connoisseur of just the right shoe. Thanks for choosing me to be your Philip Simmons.

Rossie Colter, Project Administrator for the Philip Simmons Foundation, realtor, mover and shaker, well spring of information and maker of a pretty good cup of tea. Thanks for keeping the cell phone on.

Margaret Peck & Emily Devine, Outreach and Literacy directors at St. Matthews Lutheran Church. Thanks for not being alarmed when we needed a place to rehearse and a key to get in.

Joseph "Ronnie" Pringle & Carlton Simmons. Thanks for keeping the fire burning and the iron singing.

And to the various cast members of *Sermon Of Fire*, thanks for pursuing perfection in your craft that we may continue to portray Mr. Simmons' life to many.

About The Author

Michael E. Evans

Michael E. Evans is an expert at discovering, developing, and maximizing the potential in people. A master trainer and presentations professional, Michael calls himself a M•A•P *(minister/motivator • author/artist • publisher/producer)*. His mission in life is to encourage people to Find, Follow & Finish their course.

While pastoring a local church for twelve years, Pastor Evans started seven additional churches, a publishing company, a leadership training school and an organization designed to attack the problem of racism and division in the Body of Christ. His expertise continues to benefit many industries, including Radio, Television, Film, Theater, Sales, Print Advertising, Hospitality, Education, & Government.

Michael holds a BA degree from The University of North Carolina at Chapel Hill and an honorary Ph.D. from Hosanna Bible College where he taught for two years. He also attended Word of Faith Bible College and has completed a variety of continuing education programs, including The American Management Association's Effective Executive Speaking Course.

Pastor Evans devotes his time to preaching and training, as well as writing and ghost writing for a host of others. This is his eighth book. His other titles are:

The Return Of The Lazarus Generation
What to do with the dead man at your door.
Getting Out Of Debt And Staying Out
One Nation Under Attack:
Understanding The Creation Of The Nations
A Dream Lies Dead: *A look at the dream after the death of the dreamer*
(Martin Luther King, Jr.)
The EncourageMINT *A wealth of daily inspiration, encouraging you to become who God says You Are -- In Him.*
Why?Me
Worldwide Hunger...*Is It Really Solvable?*

Pastor Evans and his wife Gloria are establishing a church, **Encouraging Word Church**, in Chapel Hill, NC. They have one daughter; Gabrielle and a grand daughter, Amaris.